THE CAR THAT SHE BUILT

The Car That She Built

Elkman, Mollie

ISBN: 979-8-218-56901-3

Let's explore 11 different skilled jobs needed to build a car!

Automotive Designer	Modeler	Mechanical Engineer
Supply Chain Manager	Prototype Engineer	Quality Control Inspector
Production Supervisor	Assembly Line Worker	Robotics Technician
Regulatory Compliance Specialist	Automotive Technician	

**This is the woman who
developed the concept.**

The Automotive Designer uses
science and art to create the shape,
size, and overall look of the car.

This is the car that she built.

**This is the woman
who created the sample.**

The Modeler uses clay and digital
design tools to make a 3D model.

This is the car that she built.

This is the woman who engineered the structure.

The Mechanical Engineer uses design and technology to make the car fast, fuel efficient, and safe.

This is the car that she built.

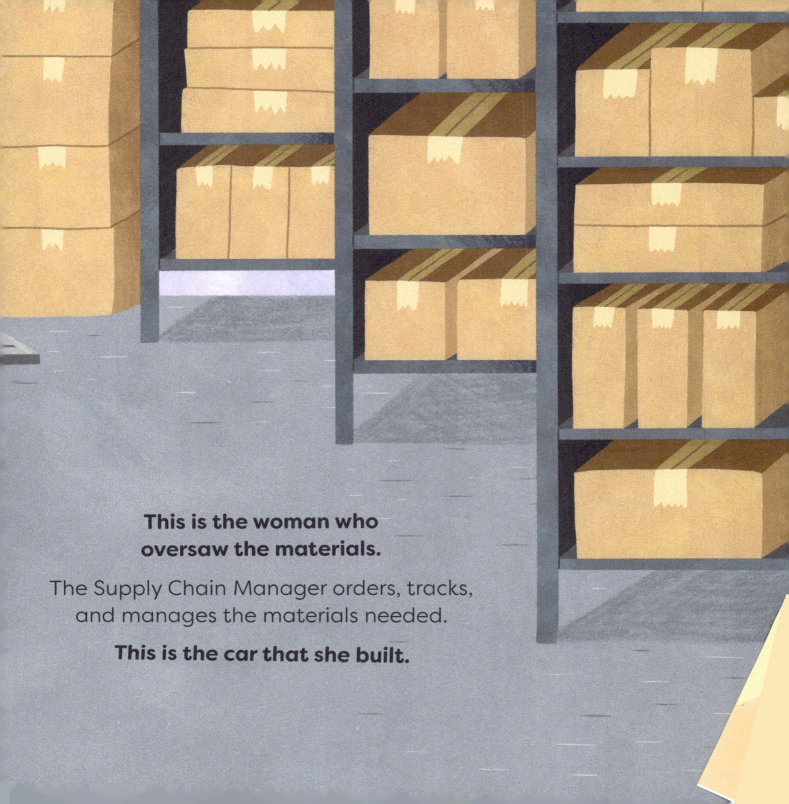

This is the woman who oversaw the materials.

The Supply Chain Manager orders, tracks, and manages the materials needed.

This is the car that she built.

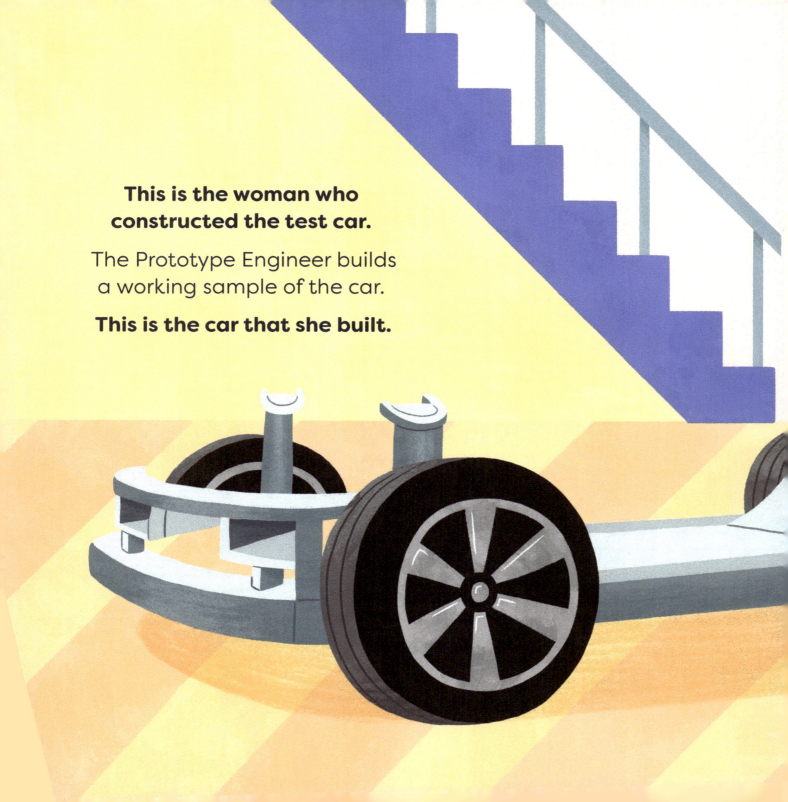

This is the woman who constructed the test car.

The Prototype Engineer builds a working sample of the car.

This is the car that she built.

This is the woman who examined the safety.

The Quality Control Inspector uses math and testing to prove that the prototype is ready to drive.

This is the car that she built.

This is the woman who managed the assembly.

The Production Supervisor helps the team work together and stay on schedule.

This is the car that she built.

SCHEDULE

		1	2	3	4	5
6	7	8	9			
13	14	15	16	17	18	19
20	21	22	23	24	25	26
27	28	29	30			

This is the woman who installed the parts.

The Assembly Line Worker connects wires, and completes important tasks to bring together the frame, body, and interior.

This is the car that she built.

This is the woman who worked with the robots.

The Robotics Technician controls the machinery that is used to build the car, and makes sure the production runs smoothly.

This is the car that she built.

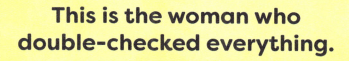

This is the woman who double-checked everything.

The Regulatory Compliance Specialist oversees final inspections to confirm that the new car meets all standards and requirements.

This is the car that she built.

This is the woman who provided care and maintenance.

The Automotive Technician conducts inspections and repairs to keep the car working and safe.

This is the car that she built.

These are the women who
are proud to say "this car is ready to drive!"
after providing care and maintenance,
double-checking everything, working with robots,
installing the parts,

overseeing the assembly, examining the safety, constructing the prototype, managing the materials, engineering the structure, creating the model, and developing the concept.

This is the car that she built.

Design Your Dream Car!